Out of Bounds

Story by Annette Smith

Illustrations by
Meredith Thomas

Rigby PM Plus Chapter Books
part of the Rigby PM Program
Ruby Level

U.S. edition © 2003 Rigby Education
A division of Reed Elsevier Inc.
1000 Hart Road
Barrington, IL 60010 - 2627
www.rigby.com

Text © 2003 Thomson Learning Australia
Illustrations © 2003 Thomson Learning Australia
Originally published in Australia by Thomson Learning Australia

All rights reserved. No part of this publication may be
reproduced or transmitted in any form or by any means,
electronic or mechanical, including photocopying, recording,
taping, or any information storage and retrieval system,
without permission in writing from the publisher.

10 9 8 7 6 5 4 3 2 1
07 06 05 04 03

Out of Bounds
    ISBN 0 75786 891 6

Printed in China by Midas Printing (Asia) Ltd

Contents

Chapter 1

Rejection

"Come on, everyone!" called Ms. Williams. "Gather around."

The children from Rooms 204 and 205 at Riverview School were staying overnight at a camp out in the country. They had been looking forward to the camp for weeks, and were very excited. This afternoon they were doing orienteering, and a concert had been planned for the evening.

"Hurry up, Falo!" yelled Greg. "We're all waiting for you."

A ripple of laughter went around the children as the new boy hurried over. Falo looked at Greg, but said nothing as he joined the others.

Ms. Williams frowned disapprovingly at Greg, then she explained the afternoon's orienteering activity. "I've put you into teams of three," she said.

Cheers went up as each group was called, and the children gathered together.

"Greg, Jon, and Falo, you'll be together, and Jane, Indira, and Sarah, you will make the final team."

Greg looked at Jon, then at Falo. "But Ms. Williams," Greg protested, "Jon and I don't want that new kid on our team. He's too fat and slow. We'll never get around the course in good time with him tagging along! Why did you put him with us?"

Falo shuffled his feet and looked away, embarrassed at the attention.

"Greg," said Ms. Williams, firmly, "that sort of attitude will not be tolerated. Falo has never done orienteering before, and he needs to be with experienced team members."

Greg scowled at Falo. He and Jon were used to winning sports activities.

"Looks like we're stuck with him then," Greg muttered.

Ms. Williams handed the cards and maps to each team. "I must remind you that the woods are out of bounds," she said. "Nobody is to go into the woods. Now Jane, your team will leave first, followed by Greg's team. A teacher will be waiting at each checkpoint to sign your cards. Right, off you go."

When Ms. Williams was out of earshot, Greg called, "Hey Falo, get over here. You need the exercise, not us." Greg and Jon smirked as Falo came over to join them.

As soon as their team was called, Greg and Jon sprinted ahead. They ran across the field toward a hill in the distance, never once slowing down to include Falo.

Falo did his best to keep up. By the time he reached the top of the steep hill, Greg and Jon were nowhere in sight. He stopped to catch his breath. Should he turn back, or just tag along with the next group who were closing in rapidly?

Just then, Greg and Jon leaped out from behind some bushes. "What kept you?" yelled Jon. "We've been here forever."

The next team waved and called out as they passed, "It looks as though you guys won't win this time! You've got a really slow team!"

Greg was beginning to get very annoyed. "I told you this would happen," he said to Jon, and then turned to Falo. "What are you going to do about it, Falo?"

"I'm doing my best," replied Falo. "It's just that you two are much faster runners than I am."

"Well, you'll have to try harder," sneered Greg, "because here comes another team!"

Chapter 2

Disobeying the Rules

In the meantime, Jon had been studying the map. "There aren't many hills after the first checkpoint. I think we could make up some time."

Greg grabbed the map. "I've got a better idea," he said. "After the first checkpoint, let's go over the ditch by the hedge, then take a shortcut through the woods to the second checkpoint. That will save us lots of time."

"But Ms. Williams said the woods are out of bounds," said Jon.

Greg shrugged. "Yeah, but that doesn't matter. She won't know. Come on. Let's keep going to the first checkpoint."

Once their card had been signed at the first checkpoint, the boys jogged on. When they were out of sight of the teacher, Greg said, "Let's have a look at the map again, Jon."

The two boys pored over the map while Falo stood nearby, waiting to see what they intended to do.

"Greg," he said at last, "I don't think we should go through the woods. That would be cheating."

"Who asked you?" retorted Greg. "Jon and I are making the decisions, not you! We've decided, haven't we Jon, that we're going to take a shortcut through the woods to make up for the time that you've lost for our team."

Jon nodded reluctantly, and the two boys set off, with Falo following as closely as he could.

13

The boys leaped over the ditch and ran on into the woods. At first they could see where they were going, but the further they went, the thicker the ferns and undergrowth became.

"Are we going in a straight line?" asked Jon. He gestured and pointed. "We came in somewhere back there, so we should probably be going that way."

"Of course we're going in a straight line," replied Greg, who didn't sound very convinced. "I'm sure we'll come out the other side soon."

"You're wrong," said Falo. "Look, we've passed that huge tree once already. I know because I recognize the creeper growing up the trunk."

"I think he's right," said Jon. "There doesn't seem to be a path, or anything that could give us an idea that we're going in the right direction. I hope we're not going around in circles!"

Chapter 3
Panic

Greg looked at his watch. "Hey! We've been in the woods for a long time. Some of the teams could be finishing by now. He glared at Falo. "If it hadn't been for you, we could have easily come in first."

"Don't blame him," said Jon. "It was our idea to take a shortcut."

Greg frowned and charged on through the undergrowth. He was furious with Jon for taking sides with Falo. But he realized they would be in trouble if they didn't find their way out soon.

"I'm not sure what we should do now," Jon said to Falo. He knew they should stay together as a group, but he also knew that if they went any further they could get really lost.

Suddenly they heard some loud cracks from breaking tree branches, and a yell from Greg as he disappeared from sight.

Jon started to run toward the place where Greg had disappeared, but Falo grabbed him by the shirt.

"Don't rush, Jon," said Falo calmly. "The ground might not be safe around here. Let me go first."

He walked carefully through the undergrowth, moving ferns and branches aside.

"Greg," he shouted, "are you all right?"

"Help! I'm down here and I've twisted my ankle," cried Greg.

Falo and Jon slid carefully down the wet slope. Greg was clutching his ankle and wincing with pain. "I don't think it's broken," he said, "but it really hurts."

Falo bent down and ran his fingers lightly over Greg's ankle. "It's hard to tell if it's broken or not," he said, "but you shouldn't try to walk on it."

"How are we going to get back?" said Jon, wishing he'd never let Greg talk him into the shortcut. He kept hearing the teacher's words: *The woods are out of bounds.*

Chapter 4
Finding a Way Out

"**I**'m going to help you, Greg," said Falo.

"What!" said Greg. "How could you help me?"

"Jon and I will get you up the slope, then I'll support you so that you don't have to put any weight on your injured ankle," replied Falo. "You think I'm fat and slow, but I'm really strong."

Greg didn't like the idea, but he didn't have any choice. Jon and Falo helped him to stand, and the three of them clambered back up to level ground.

Greg was looking very pale. "I'll see if I can walk by myself," he said, putting his foot gingerly to the ground. "I'm sure I don't need your help any more." He began to hobble then turned to the others who were looking very concerned. "It's really sore," he said. "Anyway we'd still be in this mess even if I could walk. How are we going to get out of here?"

"I'll get us out of the woods and back to the first checkpoint," said Falo quietly.

"You?" said Greg. "But Ms. Williams put you in our team because you'd never done orienteering. How can you get us back?"

"I haven't done orienteering the way you do it," said Falo, "but when I was growing up, I always went into the woods with my father and my older brothers. I know how to find my way by using the trees and ferns and grasses as signs to follow."

Greg and Jon looked at Falo in amazement. "Can you really get us out of here?" asked Greg, sounding hopeful.

"Yes," said Falo. "It won't take us too long."

"Why didn't you say so before?" said Jon. "Why did you let us get lost?"

"I wasn't lost," replied Falo with a grin. "You two were lost."

Falo pointed to a tree with creeper growing up the trunk. "Remember that tree?" he said. "We'll go in that direction. Jon, you walk ahead of us and I'll keep telling you which way to go." He put his shoulder under Greg's arm to give him support, and the three boys slowly made their way through the thick undergrowth.

Every now and then they stopped to give Greg a rest, while Falo checked marks on the ground. He looked carefully at the overhanging branches, too.

Greg and Jon didn't say much. They let Falo tell them what to do. They were feeling very bad about the way they had treated him.

It wasn't long before they were safely out of the woods, not far from where they had entered. "Phew, am I glad to be out of there!" exclaimed Jon. "Falo, I still can't believe you did it just by looking at leaves and twigs and things."

"Yeah, thanks, Falo," said Greg, "but we're going to be in real trouble when Ms. Williams finds out. Everyone must be wondering where we are. We're going to have to hurry."

"Let's just take our time and get back to the first checkpoint," said Falo. "I'll help you, Greg. The teacher who signed our card could still be there."

"Good idea," replied Jon. He pulled the crumpled map out of his pocket and grinned at Falo. "Do you trust me to get us back to the checkpoint from here?"

"Sure," laughed Falo. "I think we all know the way from here!"

Chapter 5

New Friends

When the boys finally arrived back at the first checkpoint, the teacher had left because every group had gone through some time ago.

"Should we wait here or try to get back to the camp?" asked Greg, who was shivering. "What do you think, Falo?"

"You and Jon stay here," replied Falo, with a smile. "You can put my jacket on. It's big enough! That will keep you warm. I'll go and get some help. I won't lose my way, you can be sure of that!"

Jon and Greg watched Falo jog off along the narrow track toward the brink of the hill. When he got to the top he turned, gave them a quick wave, and ran on out of sight.

Half an hour later, Falo arrived back at the checkpoint with Ms. Williams and another teacher.

"Hey, Falo, you're back!" exclaimed Jon.

"I wanted to check that you were both okay," replied Falo with a cheery grin. "I couldn't let my team mates down, could I?"

While the teachers were examining Greg's ankle, Jon said to Falo, "What did Ms. Williams say when you told her that we'd got lost in the woods?"

"I told Ms. Williams that Greg had twisted his ankle when he slipped down a muddy slope," replied Falo.

"Thanks, Falo," whispered Jon. "I don't think Greg and I will be breaking the rules again. We were very lucky this time, thanks to you."

Ms. Williams bandaged Greg's ankle, and he felt much better. The teachers took turns helping him back to the camp.

The camp concert had just begun that evening when Greg arrived back from having his ankle X-rayed in the nearest town. "It's just a sprain," he said to Jon and Falo. "Pity I can't join in the concert, though. It looks like everyone's having a good time."

"You can join in," said Falo with a huge grin on his face. "I brought my guitar. The three of us could do a song and call ourselves The Out-of-bounds Boys! What do you think, Greg?"